The NFL's Greatest Teams

SAN DIEGO CHARGERS

Big Buddy Books

An Imprint of Abdo Publishing
abdopublishing.com

Katie Lajiness

abdopublishing.com

Published by Abdo Publishing, a division of ABDO, PO Box 398166, Minneapolis, Minnesota 55439.
Copyright © 2017 by Abdo Consulting Group, Inc. International copyrights reserved in all countries. No part
of this book may be reproduced in any form without written permission from the publisher. Big Buddy Books™
is a trademark and logo of Abdo Publishing.

Printed in the United States of America, North Mankato, Minnesota.
092016
012017

THIS BOOK CONTAINS
RECYCLED MATERIALS

Cover Photo: ASSOCIATED PRESS.
Interior Photos: ASSOCIATED PRESS (pp. 5, 7, 9, 11, 13, 15, 17, 18, 19, 20, 21, 23, 25, 27, 28, 29);
    Frank Duenzl/picture-alliance/dpa/AP Images (p. 15).

Coordinating Series Editor: Tamara L. Britton
Graphic Design: Michelle Labatt, Taylor Higgins, Jenny Christensen

Publisher's Cataloging-in-Publication Data

Names: Lajiness, Katie, author.
Title: San Diego Chargers / by Katie Lajiness.
Description: Minneapolis, MN : Abdo Publishing, 2017. | Series: NFL's greatest
    teams | Includes bibliographical references and index.
Identifiers: LCCN 2016944884 | ISBN 9781680785395 (lib. bdg.) |
    ISBN 9781680798999 (ebook)
Subjects: LCSH: San Diego Chargers (Football team)--History--Juvenile
    literature.
Classification: DDC 796.332--dc23
LC record available at http://lccn.loc.gov/2016944884

Contents

A Winning Team

The San Diego Chargers are a football team from San Diego, California. They have played in the National Football League (NFL) for almost 60 years.

The Chargers have had good seasons and bad. But time and again, they've proven themselves. Let's see what makes the Chargers one of the NFL's greatest teams.

Navy, gold, and white are the team's colors.

League Play

Team Standings

The AFC and the National Football Conference (NFC) make up the NFL. Each conference has a north, south, east, and west division.

The NFL got its start in 1920. Its teams have changed over the years. Today, there are 32 teams. They make up two conferences and eight divisions.

The Chargers play in the West Division of the American Football Conference (AFC). This division also includes the Denver Broncos, the Kansas City Chiefs, and the Oakland Raiders.

Fans get excited to watch the Chargers play!

6

The Oakland Raiders have long been a rival of the Chargers.

Kicking Off

Businessman Barron Hilton founded the Chargers in 1959. The team was part of the American Football League (AFL). In 1960, the Chargers started play in Los Angeles, California. Sadly, they lost to the Houston Oilers in the AFL **championship** game.

After one year in Los Angeles, the Chargers moved to San Diego. The team enjoyed a successful 1961 season. Again, the Chargers lost the championship game to the Oilers.

In 1961, the team won 12 of 14 games.

9

Highlight Reel

Win or Go Home

NFL teams play 16 regular season games each year. The teams with the best records are part of the play-off games. Play-off winners move on to the conference championships. Then, conference winners face off in the Super Bowl!

The Chargers continued to work hard. In 1963, the team had another winning season. They went on to win their first AFL **championship**!

In 1970, the AFL joined the NFL. The Chargers struggled. Many of the team's star players had either **retired** or been traded to another team.

Paul Lowe (23) made a 46-yard touchdown run during a 1961 game against the Oakland Raiders.

In 1978, Don Coryell became head coach. He and quarterback Dan Fouts led the Chargers. The team became a powerful passing offense through 1985. During this time, the Chargers played in two conference **championship** games.

The team's best season was in 1994. They won their division and beat the Miami Dolphins in the play-offs. The Chargers went on to win the AFC championship. But, they lost to the San Francisco 49ers in the Super Bowl.

In 1995, the Chargers beat the Pittsburgh Steelers 17–13 in the AFC championship.

Halftime! Stat Break

Team Records

RUSHING YARDS
Career: LaDainian Tomlinson, 12,490 yards (2001–2009)
Single Season: LaDanian Tomlinson, 1,815 yards (2006)
PASSING YARDS
Career: Dan Fouts, 43,040 yards (1973–1987)
Single Season: Dan Fouts, 4,802 yards (1981)
RECEPTIONS
Career: Antonio Gates, 844 receptions (2003–2015)
Single Season: LaDainian Tomlinson, 100 receptions (2003)
ALL-TIME LEADING SCORER
John Carney 1,076 points, (1990–2000)

Championships

EARLY CHAMPIONSHIP WINS:
1964
SUPER BOWL APPEARANCES:
1995
SUPER BOWL WINS:
NONE

Famous Coaches

Sid Gilman (1960–1969, 1971)
Bobby Ross (1992–1996)

Pro Football Hall of Famers & Their Years with the Chargers

Lance Alworth, Wide Receiver (1962–1970)
Fred Dean, Defensive End (1975–1981)
Dan Fouts, Quarterback (1973–1987)
Sid Gillman, Coach (1960–1969, 1971)
Charlie Joiner, Wide Receiver (1976–1986)
Ron Mix, Offensive Tackle (1960–1969)
Junior Seau, Linebacker (1990–2002)
Kellen Winslow, Tight End (1979–1987)

Fan Fun

STADIUM: Qualcomm Stadium
LOCATION: San Diego, California
TEAM SONG: "San Diego Super Chargers"

Coaches' Corner

In 1960, Sid Gillman became the first head coach of the Chargers. He was the key to the team's early success. Gillman quickly built up the young team. And, he led them to win five division titles!

Bobby Ross took over the Chargers in 1992. During his five seasons with the Chargers, the team won two division titles. And, they made the play-offs three times. In 1995, Ross led the team to its first Super Bowl!

Gillman (*left*) is known as the creator of modern-day football passes.

Mike McCoy became the team's head coach in 2013.

17

Star Players

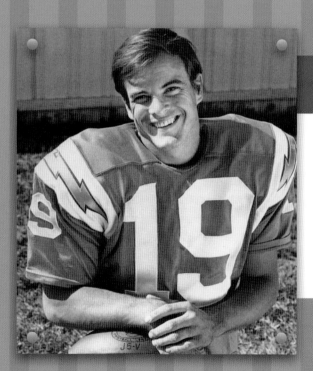

Lance Alworth WIDE RECEIVER (1962–1970)

Lance Alworth was known for his speed and graceful leaps. Alworth made 83 touchdowns with the team. And, he led the league in receiving yards and receptions three times. In 1978, Alworth became the first Chargers player to join the Pro Football Hall of Fame.

Dan Fouts QUARTERBACK (1973–1987)

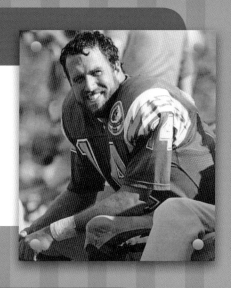

Dan Fouts helped the Chargers win three division **championships**. He led the NFL in passing yards for four straight years. Fouts was named NFL Offensive Player of the Year in 1982. During his 15 years with the Chargers, Fouts threw for 254 touchdowns!

Kellen Winslow TIGHT END (1979–1987)

Kellen Winslow played for the Chargers his entire **career**. He had a total of 541 receptions and 6,741 receiving yards. In nine seasons, Winslow made 45 touchdowns. One of his best games was a 1981 play-off win against the Miami Dolphins. In that game, he caught 13 passes for 166 yards.

Junior Seau LINEBACKER (1990–2002)

Junior Seau played with the Chargers for 13 seasons. Seau's leadership and hard work helped the team get to its first Super Bowl. In 1994, he was honored with the Walter Payton Man of the Year **award**. Seau died in 2012. He was added to the Pro Football Hall of Fame three years later.

LaDainian Tomlinson RUNNING BACK (2001–2009)

The Chargers picked LaDainian Tomlinson in the first-round of the 2001 **draft**. Tomlinson led the league in rushing twice and rushing touchdowns three times. In 2006, he won the NFL Most Valuable Player (MVP) award. The Chargers named him to the team's Hall of Fame in 2015.

Antonio Gates TIGHT END (2003–)

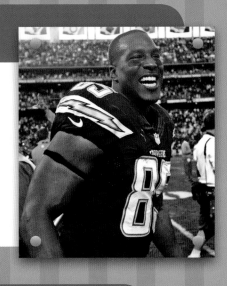

Antonio Gates has become a key player with the Chargers. His teammates voted him the Offensive Player of the Year four times. Gates is also the team's all-time leader in receptions, receiving yards, and touchdown catches. He was chosen to play in the Pro Bowl, which is the NFL's all-star game, eight times.

Philip Rivers QUARTERBACK (2004–)

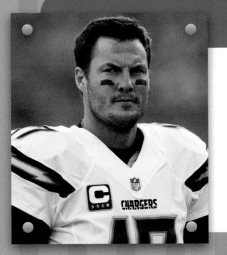

Philip Rivers joined the Chargers in 2004. Two years later, he was named starting quarterback. That season, he led the Chargers to a 14–2 record and a trip to the play-offs. Rivers holds team records for completions and passing yards. In 2013, he was named NFL Comeback Player of the Year.

Qualcomm Stadium

New Stadium?

As of 2016, there are talks to build a new Chargers stadium in San Diego.

The Chargers play home games at Qualcomm Stadium. It is in San Diego. The stadium opened in 1967. It can hold about 70,500 people.

Qualcomm Stadium hosted the Super Bowl in 1988, 1998, and 2003.

The Bolt

Thousands of fans flock to Qualcomm Stadium to see the Chargers play home games. Some fans call the Chargers the Bolt. Others sing the team song, "San Diego Super Chargers."

Boltman is a dedicated fan who dresses up to cheer on the team.

Charge!

Barron Hilton named the team the Chargers because he liked how fans yelled "Charge!" at Dodgers Stadium and University of Southern California games.

Final Call

The Chargers have a long, rich history. They played in the 1995 Super Bowl!

Even during losing seasons, true fans have stuck by them. Many believe the Chargers will remain one of the greatest teams in the NFL.

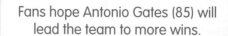

Fans hope Antonio Gates (85) will lead the team to more wins.

Through the Years

1959

Barron Hilton founds the Chargers.

1960

The team plays its first season as part of the AFL.

1964

The Chargers win the AFL **championship**.

1970

The AFL joins the NFL.

1978

Don Coryell becomes head coach.

1981

The Chargers win their third straight AFC West Division title.

1983

Dan Fouts is named Pro Bowl Most Valuable Player (MVP).

1995

The Chargers play in the Super Bowl!

1997

A record 65,714 fans attend a Chargers home game.

2016

The Chargers stay in San Diego for one more year. Then they may move to another city.

Postgame Recap

1. How many Super Bowls have the Chargers played in?
   A. 0   **B**. 1   **C**. 2

2. Name 3 of the 8 Chargers in the Pro Football Hall of Fame.

3. What is the name of the stadium where the Chargers play home games?
   A. Qualcomm Stadium
   B. Chargers Stadium
   C. San Diego Stadium

4. Which of these teams is a major rival of the Chargers?
   A. The Baltimore Ravens
   B. The Minnesota Vikings
   C. The Oakland Raiders

1. B. 2. See page 15 3. A. 4. C.

Glossary

award something that is given in recognition of good work or a good act.

career a period of time spent in a certain job.

championship a game, a match, or a race held to find a first-place winner.

draft a system for professional sports teams to choose new players.

retire to give up one's job.

Websites

To learn more about the NFL's Greatest Teams, visit **booklinks.abdopublishing.com**. These links are routinely monitored and updated to provide the most current information available.

31

Index